MW00682490

EARLY THEMES

All About Me:
Inside and Out

by Paul Oh and Ann T. Shea

SCHOLASTIC
PROFESSIONAL BOOKS

NEW YORK • TORONTO • LONDON • AUCKLAND • SYDNEY
MEXICO CITY • NEW DELHI • HONG KONG

To all the teachers in my life.
—P.O.

To my mother, Helen Shea,
whose life as a teacher inspired me
to follow that same path.
—A.S.

Edited by Joan Novelli
Cover design by Kelli Thompson
Cover art by Jo Lynn Alcorn
Interior design by Solutions by Design, Inc.
Interior illustration by Shelley Dieterichs
Poster design by Kathy Massaro
Poster illustrations by Kimberly Bulcken Root

ISBN 0-439-05009-X

Contents

About This Book

We teachers know that children are curious about their bodies. *How do I grow?* and *Why do I feel hungry?* are just two of the many questions they ask. This thematic unit responds to some of children's most common inquiries with activities that link real-life experiences to the vast world beneath their skin.

Hands-on activities and experiments will crystallize such abstract notions as how our blood circulates and why we breathe. Children will make pipe cleaner skeletons to learn about the bones in their bodies. They'll use a spray bottle and tissues to demonstrate the ways in which microscopic germs spread viruses that cause them to get sick. They'll also explore less concrete concepts about their bodies, such as their feelings and how to maintain a strong sense of self-esteem.

TEACHING WITH THEMES

When children look at the world, they don't see the artificial boundaries established in school around reading, writing, science, and math. They simply want to know more about what interests them. Teaching with themes allows you to help children pursue these interests, linking learning across the curriculum with the real world. Thematic teaching also allows children to revisit a topic over time and explore it through a variety of learning experiences, helping them gain a deeper understanding of the concepts. This is the kind

of meaningful learning that engages children and stays with them, allowing them to make connections within the unit and beyond.

You may use the activities in this book to create a thematic unit on the human body, or choose from them to supplement a unit you've been teaching for years. In either case, you can select from the following components.

- cross-curricular lessons about the human body, including hands-on experiments and extension activities

- science notes that provide background information to share with students

- suggestions for setting up and maintaining a learning center

- literature connections that link favorite nonfiction and fiction books to your science explorations

- a collaborative class banner to make and display

- ready-to-use reproducible activity pages to enhance unit lessons

- wrap-up celebration that allows your students to revisit and celebrate what they've learned through a health fair

- colorful poster, featuring the poem "Insides" by Colin West and peek-through pictures that reveal the skeletal structures of a child, a bat, a snake, and a frog

GATHERING MATERIALS

The materials you'll need for various lessons and activities in this book are generally readily available. To make managing the unit a little easier, you might want to go through the book, make a list of materials you'll need, and start gathering supplies. You might also want to enlist parents' help by sending notes home, sharing information about the theme and requesting contributions for materials you'll need. Another source for health-related materials are local doctors and medical facilities. You might request posters and other materials, and arrange to have doctors, nurses, and others in the medical profession visit your class. They might also be willing to lend medical equipment, such as stethoscopes, lab coats, crutches, slings, bandages, and so on.

SETTING UP A LEARNING CENTER

Just as its name suggests, a learning center provides a specific place where children can go to learn more about the theme. At the center, students can either work as a group or individually as they explore and gather more information for themselves. The learning center can also be a central location for storing theme materials and projects. Here are some ways you can create a Human Body

Learning Center in your classroom.

1 Set aside a space that includes a table and, preferably, a bulletin board. Post the question or topic you are studying above the bulletin board space.

2 Display books and magazines related to the theme. Check out the selections in the Literature Connections throughout this book. Encourage children to find their own books from home or the library to add to the center.

3 Organize various art supplies in bins or shoeboxes. Enlist children's help in organizing and restocking supplies after each use.

4 Display the peek-through poster in a window or hang from a clothesline.

5 Use the Learning Center Links in each section of the book to keep the center fresh and inviting.

ASSESSING STUDENT LEARNING

To keep track of students' progress, give each child a folder to decorate. You can make the folders with construction paper, or you can buy them from an office supply store. Store folders in a milk crate at the center for easy access. These folders will also come in handy when you're conferencing with parents.

USING THE JOURNAL PAGE

A decorative journal page will invite students to express ideas and information in writing and in pictures as they participate in *All About Me* activities. Make multiple copies of page 7 for each student. Students can keep their pages in a binder or folder, then staple them together at the end of the unit. Use the journal pages to give children a place to record observations and comments, and to respond to questions. For example, the activity "I Lost a Tooth!" (see page 15) invites children to record their names on a chart when they lose a tooth. Use the journal pages to go further, having children write stories about their experiences (how long the tooth was loose, what was happening when the tooth came out, and so on). You'll find that you can use the journal pages to enrich any activity in this book. Use the journals as an assessment tool. Notice how children's writing and pictures change over time, in terms of writing skills, details provided, and so on.

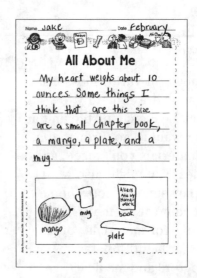

RESOURCES

Books

The Anatomy Coloring Book by Wyn Kapita and Lawrence M. Elson (HarperCollins, 1977)

Blood and Guts: A Working Guide to Your Own Insides by Linda Allison (Yolla Bolly Press, 1976)

Bones: Our Skeletal System by Seymour Simon (Morrow, 1998)

How the Body Works: 100 Ways Parents and Kids Can Share the Miracle of the Body by Steve Parker (Reader's Digest Association, 1994)

Muscles: Our Muscular System by Seymour Simon (Morrow, 1998). Other titles in the series include *The Heart: Our Circulatory System* and *The Brain: Our Nervous System*.

The Skeleton Inside You by Philip Balestrino (HarperCollins, 1989)

The Visual Dictionary of the Human Body (Dorling Kindersley, 1991)

Software

My Amazing Human Body (DK Multimedia)

The Magic School Bus Explores the Human Body (Microsoft)

Video

NotesAlive! (Minnesota Orchestra, 612-371-7123): This music-based program includes a wonderful video version of Dr. Seuss's *Many Colored Days*, a rich resource for a study of the five senses.

Web Sites

The Virtual Body: **www.medtropolis.com/vbody**

Bill Nye the Science Guy's Nye Labs Online: **www.nyelabs.com/flash_go**

Yuckiest Site on the Internet: **www.nj.com/yucky/index.html**

All About Me

_____

_____

_____

_____

_____

Early Themes: All About Me Scholastic Professional Books

Launching the Theme

To kick off any unit, it's helpful to find out what students already know. This encourages children to set learning goals, and it helps you plan lessons accordingly. Use the following set of KWL (What I Know, What I Want to Know, What I Learned) activities to introduce your thematic unit on the human body. Let students' responses guide the activities you select and the order in which you present them.

Materials

- ◎ KWL Record Sheet (see page 9)
- ◎ craft paper
- ◎ scissors
- ◎ markers, pencils

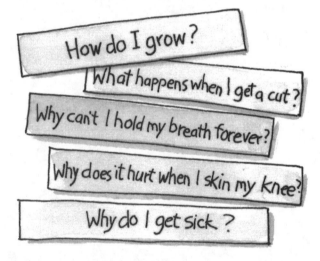

How do I grow?

What happens when I get a cut?

Why can't I hold my breath forever?

Why does it hurt when I skin my knee?

Why do I get sick?

What I Know

I need food to grow.

Write each of the big questions covered in this unit on a sentence strip and display them. Read them aloud with children and ask: *What do you already know about these questions?* Make a class set of page 9, and give each child a copy. Have children use the record sheets to write down things they know about the questions. Label a sheet of chart paper *What I Know*.

Have children take turns taping up their KWL record sheets to show what they know.

What I Want to Know

How big is my heart?

Display a second sheet of chart paper and label it *What I Want to Know*. Give students a second copy of page 9 and have them record things they would like to learn. Have them tape these record sheets to the chart.

What I Learned

I have to sleep when my body is tired.

Complete this section at the conclusion of the unit. Give students additional copies of page 9 and let them record things they've learned. Students can tape these record sheets to a third chart labeled *What I Learned*.

TIP: Rather than create one set of KWL charts for all of the sections of this book, you may want to create separate sets of charts for each section. Either way, this approach will provide a wonderful record of students' growth.

KWL Record Sheet

How Do I Grow?

Children know that they get bigger. When they go to the doctor, they discover just how much they've grown since their last visit. They might even see a growth chart. But rarely is the time taken to show them exactly why and how that change occurs. In this section, children will look at how they've changed since they were babies. They'll learn about bones and teeth, find out exactly what fuels those growth spurts they all hear about, and more.

SCIENCE NOTES

Bones are alive: They take in food, grow, and heal when they break. About 30 percent of bone is living tissue. The outside layer, though, is the part that requires calcium in order to create a hard surface. When you are born, your bones are soft. As you age, they *ossify*, or harden. Bones need many things to grow and stay healthy, including Vitamin D and calcium, which can be found in dairy products, as well as in other foods.

10

Watch Me Change!

Photographs and stories from home help your students understand just how much they've changed since they were babies.

Materials

◎ photos or drawings of each student from different life stages

◎ tape

◎ construction paper (long strips)

Teaching the Lesson

1. Invite students to bring in pictures of themselves at different times in their lives—for example, as a baby, as a toddler, and as a preschooler. Ask parents to guide children in recording a sentence about the stage/photo.

TIP: Because not all children will be able to bring in photos of themselves, be sure to suggest that they can also draw pictures of themselves at different ages.

2. Have students carefully tape the photos to construction paper (loop the tape and stick it on the back of the pictures) in chronological order. Above each picture, have them record their age. Below each picture, have children copy the sentence that tells something about that age. Tell them they've just created a time line of their lives!

1 year	3 years	5 years	7 years
I can walk	I went down the slide	I can read a book	I can ride a two-wheeler

3. Invite children to share their time lines. Encourage them to make comparisons among the different photographs. *How have they changed? How have they stayed the same?* (Students might compare hair, height, eye color, smiles, and so on. They may notice photos that show missing teeth. They might also compare things they can do at each stage, such as crawling, walking, riding a bike, and so on.)

4. Guide students in understanding that as they grow older, their bodies change. They look different in some ways and are able to do different things. In the next few activities, students will explore how those changes occur.

Literature Connection The book *How Kids Grow* by Jean Marzollo (Scholastic, 1998) uses lovely photographs to show how children change from birth to age seven. It also points out what many children are capable of doing at different stages in life. After reading the book, invite children to share memories of some of their firsts—for example, the first time they could ride a two-wheeler or read a book.

ACTIVITY Extension Invite parents and grandparents to visit with your students and share stories about their childhoods. Encourage them to bring in photos. Have students brainstorm in advance questions about their guests' childhoods.

Learning Center Link

Label six pieces of posterboard as follows: Infant, Toddler, Young Child, Teen, Adult, Senior. Provide magazines, scissors, and glue. Have children cut out pictures from the magazines of people at different stages of life and paste them on the corresponding posters. Take time to visit with children and talk with them about how they know where the pictures belong.

Them Bones

Students learn about human bones and make their own "skeletons."

Materials

- ◎ *The Skeleton Inside You* by Philip Balestrino (HarperCollins, 1989)
- ◎ construction paper (18 by 24 inches)
- ◎ pipe cleaners
- ◎ glue

Teaching the Lesson

1. Read *The Skeleton Inside You* with students. Point out that inside each child are bones. Have students feel the bones in their arms and hands, then describe them.

2. Give students time to study the picture of the human skeleton in the book. Share other resources on the human skeleton, too.

3. Give each student a handful of pipe cleaners to bend and connect in the shape of a human skeleton.

4. Have students glue the pipe cleaner skeleton to the construction paper. Invite them to label some of the bones, such as the skull, vertebrae (backbone), and rib cage.

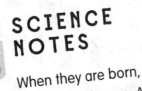

SCIENCE NOTES

When they are born, children have more than 300 bones. As they grow older, some of their bones fuse together so that by the time they become adults, they have only about 200 bones!

5. Display the skeletons on the bulletin board at your Human Body Learning Center. Follow up by discussing how children's bones will change as they grow older. Surprise them with this fact: They have about 100 more bones than you do!

Literature Connection
Share *The Teeny Tiny Woman* by Jane O'Connor (Random House, 1986) with your students. They'll enjoy chiming in as you read, supplying the voice throughout the story that says, "Give me my bone!"

ACTIVITY Extension
Pair up students and have them measure bones on their bodies. They can use tape measures or nontraditional measures, such as string. Before you begin, go over the names of bones they are likely to measure—for example, the *femur* (thigh), the *tibia* (shinbone), the *humerus* (upper arm), and the *skull*. Make a class chart listing each student's measurements. Ask questions to guide a discussion—for example, *What is the range of lengths of the femur bone in our class? How big around is the smallest skull in our class? The largest? About how big do you think the average skull is?*

Learning Center Link

Post chart paper. At the top write the word bone. *As children visit the learning center, invite them to add words that rhyme with* bone, *such as* stone, cone, phone, tone, *and* alone. *Encourage children to read the words aloud, noticing which letters in the words sound the same.*

My Incredible Insides

Use the peek-through poster to give students a broader understanding of the internal structures of all animals, and give them a chance to compare their insides with those of a bat, a snake, a frog, and a pigeon.

Materials

- "Insides" peek-through poetry poster (see center of book)
- craft paper (5 by 2 feet)
- scissors
- markers, crayons, paint
- human body reference materials

Teaching the Lesson

1. Before displaying the poster, show students the skeleton side and invite them to guess who each skeleton belongs to. Hold the poster up to a light source to reveal the illustrations on the reverse and read aloud the poem. Allow time for children to respond to the last two lines: "I do so hate to think about what I would look like inside-out."

2. Let children brainstorm things they think they have in common with the animals on the poster, and the things that are different. Ask: *Are there some body parts that all animals have? Why do you think that? What makes a snake able to slither? How do you think that frogs are able to breathe under water? What makes you and a bat alike? How are you like a pigeon?*

3. Let students work with partners to trace the outlines of their own bodies on craft paper.

4. Have children cut out their silhouettes and fill them in with drawings that represent different parts of the human body. In addition to bones, they might include lungs, the heart, the digestive tract, and so on. Students can add captions to tell more.

TIP: Provide a variety of resources to assist students with this activity. See Resources, page 6, for suggestions.

Literature Connection Read aloud *Stellaluna* by Janell Cannon (Harcourt Brace, 1993). In this heartwarming story, a bat learns that in spite of their love and friendship he is different from the birds who adopt him. He discovers in the end that it's okay to be different. Have children make puppets to act out the story. They might make the bat puppets two-sided—one showing the external features of a bat, the other showing the internal structure.

ACTIVITY Extension Invite students to work with partners to find out what the insides of other animals look like. Have them draw pictures of both the outside and inside of the animals they choose. Mix up the pictures and let students try to match each animal's insides and outsides.

Learning Center Link

Copy the poster poem on sentence strips. Cut apart each word. Display in a pocket chart. Let children refer to the poster to put the poem back together. Provide blank cards on which children can record words that rhyme with rhyming words in the poem (skin/in, about/out).

What's for Lunch?

Children discover what their bodies need in order to grow by examining their lunches and classifying the foods they eat into the different nutritional groups.

SCIENCE NOTES

Your body uses food as energy. The food is broken down into smaller and smaller pieces until it is tiny enough to flow through your blood and into the cells that comprise your body.

Materials

- ◎ letter to families (see page 16)
- ◎ chart paper
- ◎ scissors
- ◎ yarn
- ◎ crayons and markers
- ◎ lunch
- ◎ What's for Lunch? chart (see page 17)

Teaching the Lesson

1. Send home a note explaining that children will be taking a closer look at the foods they eat. (You can copy the ready-to-use note on page 16 or make your own.) As part of the lesson, they will be examining the foods they eat for lunch one day. Note the day that students will be doing this activity so that parents can plan ahead. (They may choose to pack lunches or have their children eat the cafeteria meal.)

2. Introduce the activity by asking children what they think it means to be a healthy eater. Record and discuss comments.

3. Prior to the class lunch, explain that food is used by children's bodies to help them grow. Draw a picture of the food pyramid and let students volunteer foods that fit into each category: fruits/vegetables, grains, meat/fish/dairy/soy, and fats/sweets.

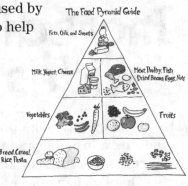

4. During lunch on the selected day, have everyone eat in the classroom. Before students begin eating, have them take a close look at their lunches. Give each child a copy of the "What's for Lunch?" chart to complete.

5. After lunch, have children share their charts. Ask: *Is there a food you might want to eat less of? More of?* Write a class letter to families about the findings.

ACTIVITY Extension Have students make interactive place mats to be used in the classroom during snack time. Using a piece of construction paper, they can draw a large circle for each section of the food pyramid. Inside the circles, ask them to draw examples of foods that make up that group. Laminate the place mats so they can be washed and re-used. Children can categorize their snacks by placing them in the appropriate circles.

Literature Connection To give your children a mouthwatering accompaniment to their lunchtime discoveries, read *Hold the Anchovies* by Shelley Rotner and Julia Pemberton Hellums (Orchard Books, 1996). You might ask children to list the food groups included in the book as you read. At the end, you'll find a recipe for making a delicious pizza!

SCIENCE/MATH

I Lost a Tooth!

Children enjoy keeping track of how many teeth they've lost, and at this age they can lose many! Create and keep Tooth-Tracking Charts that stay up over the course of the year to make math and science connections when students lose their teeth.

Materials

◉ tooth template (see page 18)

Teaching the Lesson

1 Make one copy of the tooth template for each month of the school year (or for as many months as there are left in the year). Display the tooth-shaped record sheet. Put the name of the month at the top. Explain that the class will keep track of how many teeth students lose during this month.

2 Ask if anyone has lost a tooth this month. Have students who answer *yes* come up to the tooth-shaped record sheet and fill in their names on one of the blank lines. (Eliminate this step if you start the activity on the first of the month.)

3 Post the record sheet in a place that is accessible to students. (The classroom door is a good spot and will invite students to notice changes on the charts each day.) As students lose teeth during the month, have them write their names on the record sheet.

4 At the end of the month, have children count the names on the record sheet and complete the sentence at the bottom.

5 Use the charts to make quick math connections. For example, ask: *During which month did the most children lose teeth? During which month did the fewest children lose teeth? How many more teeth were lost in [month] than in [month]? Who has lost the most teeth so far this year?*

ACTIVITY Extension Discuss which teeth students lost each month. Display a diagram of a child's mouth with teeth labeled. (A local dentist may be able to provide one.) Try a simple investigation to learn more. Give each child an apple slice or celery stick. (Check for allergies first.) Have them eat the snack, noticing which teeth they use for biting and which teeth they use for chewing. Go further by discussing how the number of teeth students have changes over time. Let students guess how many teeth they'll have at different ages, then share this information: New baby: 0 teeth; age 1: 12 teeth; age 2: 20 teeth; age 6: 24 teeth; age 12: 28 teeth; age 18: 32 teeth.

Literature Connection Many of your students may be familiar with the tooth fairy tradition. Learn about other tooth traditions with *Throw Your Tooth on the Roof: Tooth Traditions from Around the World* by Selby B. Beeler (Houghton Mifflin, 1998). Follow up by displaying a world map on your wall or bulletin board. Let children mark the places on the map that correspond to the places in the book, then write captions (or draw pictures) that tell about the traditions.

Name_____ Date_____

Dear Families,

As part of a science unit on the human body, your child is investigating foods that fuel his or her growth. On _____, your child will be taking a close look at his or her lunch. Your child will chart the different kinds of foods in the lunch (fruits/vegetables, grains, meat/fish/dairy/soy, fats/sweets). We'll look at the food pyramid to discover how the foods we eat fit into a healthy diet. If you are packing your child's lunch on this day, please keep this in mind. Thank you for your help with this project!

Sincerely,

Your Child's Teacher

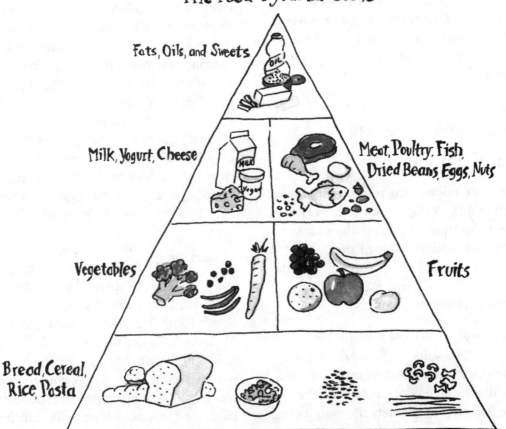

The Food Pyramid Guide

Fats, Oils, and Sweets

Milk, Yogurt, Cheese

Meat, Poultry, Fish, Dried Beans, Eggs, Nuts

Vegetables

Fruits

Bread, Cereal, Rice, Pasta

Early Themes: All About Me Scholastic Professional Books

Name_____ Date_____

What's for Lunch?

Draw pictures in the lunchbox to show the foods in your lunch.

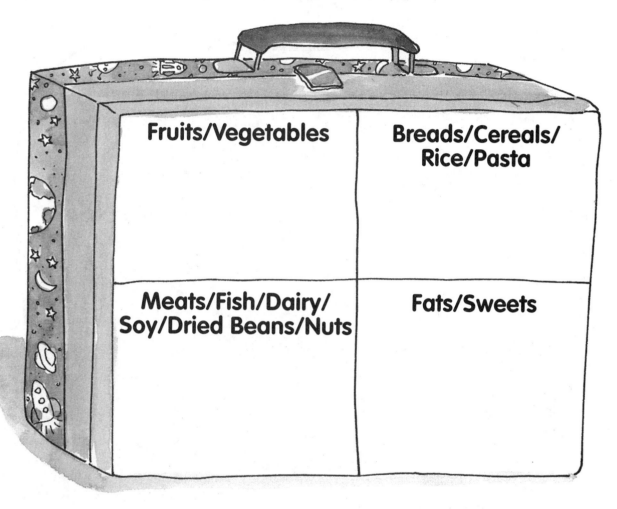

| Fruits/Vegetables | Breads/Cereals/Rice/Pasta |
| Meats/Fish/Dairy/Soy/Dried Beans/Nuts | Fats/Sweets |

Color the picture to show how you feel about the lunch you ate.

I Lost a Tooth!

Month _____

During the month of _____,
_____ students lost _____ teeth all together!

Early Themes: All About Me   Scholastic Professional Books

What Happens When I Get a Cut?

I *'ve got a cut!* **How many times each day do your students ask if they can go to the nurse for a bandage? Even the tiniest of scrapes is cause for children to request a trip to the nurse—often a favorite school destination! In this group of activities, your** students will learn what's behind the blood they see when they get a cut: their circulatory systems. They'll also make a stethoscope to listen to their heartbeats, and find their pulse to discover how rapidly their heart beats.

SCIENCE NOTES

Explain to children that their hearts are always beating, and their blood is always moving: This is their circulatory system. Blood carries oxygen throughout their bodies. The oxygen helps all the parts of the body to do their work. When children get a cut, some of the blood that is flowing through their capillaries (tiny blood vessels) squeezes out of their skin, which is a protective covering for all their blood vessels.

The Beat Goes On

Students make stethoscopes to learn more about the way their hearts work.

Materials

- ◎ picture of a stethoscope (or a real stethoscope)
- ◎ paper towel tubes (one for each student)
- ◎ chart paper

SCIENCE NOTES

Your heart is a muscle that is about the size of your fist. Blood that enters your heart from your lungs is filled with oxygen, and then sent on a long journey throughout your body. Blood that needs oxygen is pumped from the heart to the lungs. There are three types of blood vessels, or tubes, that carry blood: *arteries, veins,* and *capillaries.* Arteries carry blood from the heart to other parts of the body. Veins carry blood to the heart and lungs. Capillaries are the tiniest blood vessels, each finer than a hair. They carry blood to all the farthest reaches of the body. End to end, your body's blood vessels would measure about 60,000 miles!

Teaching the Lesson

1. Ask students to open one of their hands. Then have them close it into a fist. Have them repeat this several times. Explain that this is similar to what their hearts do: When their fist closes, it is like the heart pushing blood out and sending it on a journey throughout the body. When their fist opens, it is like blood flowing into their heart. (The heart does this about 100,000 times a day.)

2. Ask students if a doctor has ever listened to their heartbeat. Ask: *Does anyone know the name of the tool a doctor uses to listen to the heart?* (stethoscope) Display a picture of a stethoscope or, if possible, show a real one.

3. Have children use the paper towel tubes like stethoscopes, decorating them first, if desired. Let them team up with partners, then put one end to their ears and one to each of these places:

- ◎ the palm of one hand
- ◎ a knee
- ◎ a foot
- ◎ the back near a shoulder
- ◎ the chest, just to the left of the middle

4. Invite children to describe what they heard. Ask: *Where was it easiest to hear a heartbeat?* Divide a piece of craft paper into five sections. Draw and label a picture on the chart of each place children checked. Let children record their responses to make a scatter chart. (Children should discover that it is easiest to hear the heartbeat in the last position: *chest.*)

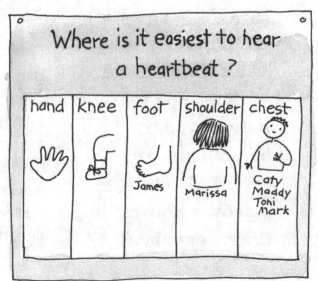

Literature Connection

In *Dr. Cat* by Harriet Ziefert (Viking, 1989), three little kittens visit a doctor's office and are put at ease by the kindly Dr. Cat, who lets them use a stethoscope on him before he uses it on them. This might be a good opportunity to explore children's feelings about going to the doctor. *What are some things that worry them about going to a doctor? What are some ways their doctors help them feel at ease?*

ACTIVITY Extension

Display a picture of the heart from a book, such as *The Heart: Our Circulatory System* by Seymour Simon (William Morrow, 1996). Follow up by letting students make clay models.

Learning Center Link

Borrow some tools from a doctor and leave them out for children to explore. You might ask for a lab coat, a stethoscope, tongue depressors, bandages, and X rays.

MATH

Faster, Slower

Asleep or awake, your blood is continually pulsing through your veins and arteries. The following activity demonstrates this process to students, including the fact that the blood flow can speed up and slow down.

Materials

- My Pulse record sheet (see page 24)
- timer (or clock with minute hand)

SCIENCE NOTES

Guide students to understand that when they exercise, their pulse quickens because their heart is forced to pump more blood to the muscles that are moving. Different animals have different pulse rates. A mouse's heart, for example, beats 500 times a minute. An elephant, on the other hand, has a pulse rate of 25 times per minute. A rabbit's heart beats about 200 times a minute.

Teaching the Lesson

1 Review what students learned in "The Beat Goes On." (See page 20.) Explain that another way to discover their heart working is to find their pulse. Guide children in placing two fingers on the side of their neck, or on the inside of their wrist, to feel their pulse. Point out that what they feel is their heart pushing blood through tubes called *blood vessels*. (See Science Notes, page 20.)

2 Ask: *When you play tag or jump rope or exercise in another way, what happens to your heart?* Explain that exercise gives their heart a workout. When they exercise, their pulse quickens. (See Science Notes, above)

3 Have children find their pulse and count a few beats. Give each child a copy of the record sheet. Ask: *How many times do you think your heart beats in one minute?* Have students

My Pulse
Before Exercise
I estimate that my heart beats _____ times in one minute.
My heart really beats _____ times in one minute.
After Exercise
I estimate that my heart will beat _____ times in one minute after I exercise.
My heart really beat _____ times in one minute after I exercised.
My heart beats FASTER SLOWER after I exercise. (circle one)
This is why I think this happens.
_____
_____
_____
_____
On the back of this paper, draw a picture that shows you exercising.
24

record an estimate on the record sheet under "Before Exercise" then take their pulse while you time them for one minute. (You can also time them for 30 seconds and have them double the number.) Have students record their actual pulse rate on their chart.

4 Ask students to estimate what their pulse rate will be after exercising for one minute and record the estimate under "After Exercise." Have them run in place, or do jumping jacks, as you time them for one minute, then record their actual pulse rate.

5 Bring students together to discuss pulse rates before and after exercising. Were they surprised by the results? Invite children to offer explanations for pulse rates going up after exercising. (See Science Notes, page 21.)

Literature Connection
The circulatory system is like a big circle. The heart pumps blood with oxygen throughout the body and, when the oxygen is used up, the blood travels back to the lungs to get more oxygen and the circle continues. Teach students this traditional song about circles and continuity.

Make New Friends

Make new friends
But keep the old,
One is silver and the other's gold.
A circle is round,
It has no end
That's how long I want to be your friend.

 ACTIVITY Extension
Have students record their pulse rate after other activities, such as sitting, standing, walking, writing, and so on. In each case, time the activity for one minute. Which activity makes their heart beat faster? (Make sure to allow time between activities for students' pulse rates to return to normal.) To go further, ask students to predict who will have a higher pulse rate: a child or an adult. Have them devise a test to find out.

 ## Learning Center Link

Discuss the need to keep the muscles in our bodies strong. Guide children in understanding that the heart is one of those muscles. Let children collaborate on a Healthy Hearts mural to learn more. Post craft paper on a wall. Stock a nearby desk with markers, crayons, colored pencils, and other art supplies. Invite children to add pictures and words to the mural to show how they keep their hearts healthy—for example, by walking to school, playing tag at recess, raking leaves after school, riding a bike, and so on.

ART/WRITING

A Big Heart

In science, the heart is a muscle that pumps blood throughout the body. But in art and literature, the heart is used to symbolize traits such as love, generosity, honor, and courage. In this activity, your students will listen to a story about a small, courageous tiger, then share times they've been brave, too.

Materials

- *Heart of a Tiger* by Marsha Diane Arnold (Dial, 1995)
- heart-shaped template (see page 25)
- scissors
- glue sticks
- pencils
- markers

Learning Center Link

Take the heart cards out of several decks of playing cards. Post directions for this card game. Let children make up their own games to play, too.

- ◎ *Each player puts down two cards, face up, then adds the hearts on both cards. (For younger students, one card might be sufficient.)*
- ◎ *The person with the higher number of hearts takes the four cards. If the total is the same, each player places two more cards down, and so on, until one person has a higher total.*
- ◎ *The game is over when one player has all the cards.*

Teaching the Lesson

1. Read the book *Heart of a Tiger*, a story about the smallest cub in a litter who needs to find a name for himself before Naming Day. The cub doesn't want to be called "Smallest of All," and is finally named "Heart of a Tiger" after saving the life of Bengal, a large, beautiful tiger.

2. Discuss what it means to be brave. Tell students that often people describe someone who is brave as having a "big heart." Ask them to think of times they've been brave.

3. Give each child a copy of the heart template. Let children use the template to write and illustrate stories about their acts of bravery. (Children can use multiple copies of the template to make heart-shaped mini-books.)

4. Display the hearts on the Human Body bulletin board, or suspend them from the ceiling or a string across the room.

Literature Connection The book *The Crystal Heart: A Vietnamese Legend* by Aaron Shephard (Atheneum, 1998) tells the story of a girl whose cruelty turns a fisherman's heart to crystal. However, her tears of sorrow at this act ultimately set him free. After reading the story, have children complete this sentence about themselves: *My heart is like a heart of _____.* Possible answers to discuss might be a *tiger*, *crystal*, *lion*, *stone*, *water*, *air*, the *sun*, and so on.

ACTIVITY Extension Have students go on a scavenger hunt for hearts at home. They might find them in signs, advertisements on television, their personal belongings, and so on. Have children list (or draw pictures) of places they see hearts, then bring their findings to school. Discuss and compare results. Tally the number of places students saw the heart symbol used. You can do this by setting up a chart and having children place heart-shaped stickers on it as they share their lists.

SCIENCE NOTES

Contrary to the expression "big heart," the heart is quite small—about the size of your fist. Your students may be interested to know that their hearts weigh approximately ten ounces. Weigh an object to give students something to compare this information with. A sneaker, for example, might weigh about ten ounces.

Name_____ Date _____

My Pulse

Before Exercise

I estimate that my heart beats _____ times in one minute.

My heart really beats _____ times in one minute.

After Exercise

I estimate that my heart will beat _____ times in one minute after I exercise.

My heart really beat _____ times in one minute after I exercised.

My heart beats FASTER SLOWER after I exercise. (circle one)

This is why I think this happens.

_____

_____

_____

_____

_____

_____

On the back of this paper, draw a picture that shows you exercising.

Early Themes: All About Me Scholastic Professional Books

Heart Template

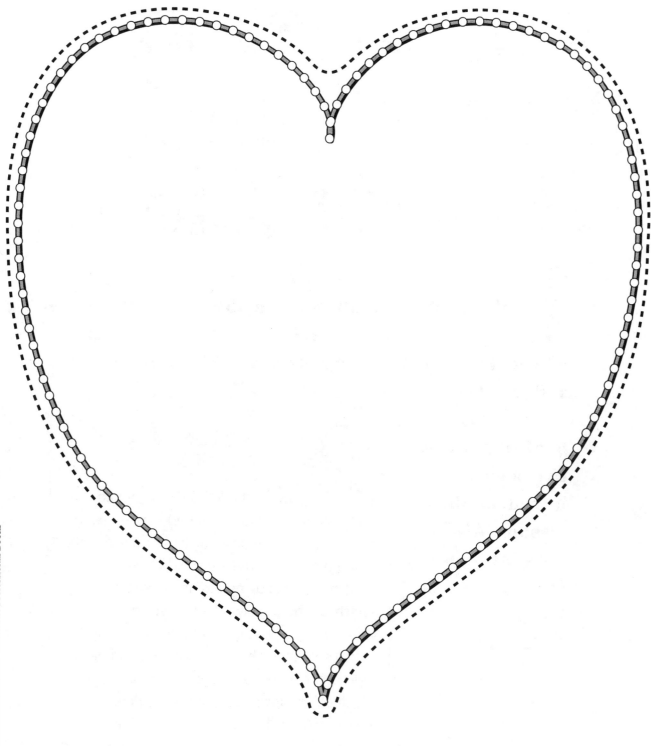

Why Does It Hurt When I Skin My Knee?

In this section children learn about the five senses that allow them to see, hear, smell, taste, and yes, feel pain. After completing a KWL chart with children (see page 8), share a book about the five senses to introduce the lessons. Aliki's *My Five Senses* (HarperCollins Publishers, 1962) is a good choice.

SCIENCE NOTES

The five senses—touch, taste, sight, smell, and hearing—are how our bodies tell our brains what is happening in the world around us. The senses do this by sending signals along the nervous system, which is a huge network of nerve cells called *neurons* that spreads throughout the body. Touch something hot, for example, and nerve cells at the tip of your finger quickly send an electrical impulse along the network to your brain, which tells you what you are feeling.

Five Senses Stations

Set up stations to explore the five senses. You can set aside a block of time for children to rotate through each station, or plan to have each group do one station a day over a week's time. To make a Five Senses Learning Log, copy a class set of pages 29 and 30. Give each child a set of pages. Have children cut apart their pages, add a cover and staple to bind. Have children record information in their learning logs at teach station.

STATION 1
No Hands!

Children discover just how much information their sense of touch provides. You'll need mittens, a box with a lid, and some touchable items for this station.

◎ Cut a fist-sized hole in the side of a box. Drape a piece of cloth over the hole. Staple or tape the cloth to the top of the box so that it stays in place.

◎ Place a mystery object in the box, such as a small ball, dice, a toy car, an eraser, and so on.

◎ Have children put a mitten on one hand, then touch the object in the box. Have children guess what the object is and record this in their learning logs.

◎ Let children remove the mitten and try again, recording the new guess in the log. Repeat the activity for several objects. Have children tell which was easier: guessing the object with or without the mitten.

STATION 2
Match That Sound

Students become "sound detectives" to learn more about the sense of hearing.

◎ Fill two empty film canisters partway with popcorn kernels, two with marbles, two with sugar, and so on. Prepare ten canisters in this way (five sets of two) Number the canister tops randomly from one to ten.

◎ Have children shake the canisters and try to determine which ones match. Have children record the numbers of matching canisters in their learning logs.

◎ Let children share their findings. Are there any disagreements as to which canisters match? Shake them for everyone to hear and let students revise their guesses. Reveal the canister contents in sets.

Literature Connection Discuss the idea that when people are unable to hear, it affects how they communicate. Share *The Handmade Alphabet* by Laura Rankin (Scholastic, 1991) to learn about sign language as a way for people who are hearing-impaired to communicate with others. Let students learn more about their sense of hearing with *Owl Moon* by Jane Yolen (Philomel, 1987), the story of a young girl who goes out at night with her father to listen for owls. After reading the book, take children outside or to another location in the school and have them sit quietly. Let them close their eyes and listen for sounds.

STATION 3
Color My World

Colors are an important part of our sense of sight. At this station children explore their sense of sight

as they compose color poems. Set up for this station by making a class set of the poem on page 31. Have chart paper handy, as well as crayons, markers, and pencils.

◎ Before sharing the poem "Yellow," ask children to name things that are yellow. Write them on chart paper. Then ask them to listen for those things and more as you read aloud the poem.

◎ Have children complete page 3 of their learning log to write their own color poems. Let them draw pictures to go with their poems.

◎ Let children take their copies of the poem "Yellow" home to share with their families. Activities on this page invite families to play with colors and poetry together.

| Literature Connection | In *The Seeing Stick* by Jane Yolen (Crowell, 1977), a blind princess, Hwei Ming, learns to see through her sense of touch with the help of a wise old man. In the end, she is finally able to "see" her father's face.

STATION 4
Taste and Smell Work Together

Prepare several snacks, such as orange slices, apple slices, and potato sticks. Set the plates on a table. Fold a couple of large sheets of cardboard, then open them up and set on the table to conceal the snacks.

◎ Blindfold children at this station. Have them pinch their noses and taste each food. Ask them to tell you what they think

it is. Have students record their guesses in the log.

◎ Repeat the activity with noses not pinched. Have students record their guesses again.

◎ Help children recognize that their sense of smell is linked to their sense of taste.

SAFETY TIP: Check for food allergies before setting up this station.

| Literature Connection | You can almost smell and taste the bread in *Bread, Bread, Bread* by Ann Morris (Morrow, 1993). Take a survey of students' favorite breads and display results in a picture graph.

| ACTIVITY Extension | Cut out sensory-rich pictures from magazines. Choose pictures that have people in them. Glue them to posterboard, leaving plenty of space between pictures. Have children use symbols for each sense (eyes, hands, mouth, nose, ears) to record which senses the people in each picture could be using. You might have students work in small groups for this activity. (Make one set of pictures for each group.)

Learning Center Link

Make a blank book by stapling sturdy paper together. Provide magazines from which students can cut out pictures. Have children paste pictures of people involved in different activities (eating, swimming, buying something at a bakery, walking a dog, and so on) in the book. Have them tell what senses the people are using in each picture.

Station 1: No Hands!

	With a Mitten	Without a Mitten
Mystery Object 1		
Mystery Object 2		
Mystery Object 3		

(1)

Station 2: Match That Sound

My Matches	What I Think Is Inside	What Is Inside
___ and ___		
___ and ___		
___ and ___		
___ and ___		
___ and ___		

(2)

29

Station 3: Color My World

_____'s Color Poem

What is _____?

_____

_____

_____

_____

These things are _____!

Draw a picture to go with your poem.

③

Station 4: Taste and Smell Work Together

	Nose Pinched	Nose Not Pinched
Mystery Food 1		
Mystery Food 2		
Mystery Food 3		

④

Yellow

Green is go,
and red is stop
and yellow is peaches
with cream on top.

Earth is brown,
and blue is sky;
yellow looks well
on a butterfly.

Clouds are white,
black, pink, or mocha;
yellow's a dish of
tapioca.

—David McCord

Try This!

◎ Find two words in the poem that rhyme with **hop**. Play a rhyming game. Take turns naming more words that rhyme with **hop**. Play until you run out of words or time.

◎ Go on a scavenger hunt at home. Can you find 10 things that are yellow? How many more can you find? Make a list!

◎ Make up your own poem about a favorite color. Your words don't have to rhyme.

Early Themes: All About Me Scholastic Professional Books

Why Do I Get Sick?

Being sick is no fun. Are there ways to keep it from happening? In this section your students will discover what germs are and how our bodies protect us from them, and learn how to prevent those germs from spreading in the first place.

SCIENCE NOTES

Germs are tiny organisms (also called *pathogens*) that can make the body sick by invading its cells. Luckily, you have a defense called the *immune system*, made up primarily of white blood cells, which float along in your blood vessels. These bodyguards attack and destroy invading germs. However, if your immune system is weak, or if there are an overwhelming number of germs, your body may not be able to keep those germs from making you sick.

When I Feel Yucky

Sometimes, no matter how hard you try to prevent it, you still get sick. Have your students write poems that express what it's like for them when they're not feeling well.

Materials

◎ chart paper

Teaching the Lesson

1. Ask students to think about times when they've been sick. Brainstorm words that describe how they've felt at those times. Record their words on chart paper.

2. Write this poem starter on chart paper:

When I feel yucky I _____.

When I feel yucky I _____.

When I feel yucky I _____.

And the only thing that makes me feel
  better is _____.

3. Complete the poem as a class. Then have children copy the poem starter and fill in the blanks with new words to make their own poems.

4. Invite children to share their poems, then bind them to make a class book.

Literature Connection In *I Wish I Was Sick, Too* by Franz Brandenberg (Mulberry, 1990), a young girl envies the attention her sick brother receives until she gets sick, too! Ask your students how they feel when a family member is sick. What are some ways they would help someone feel better?

SCIENCE NOTES

Have students look at one another's throats. Explain that usually their throats are dark pink. When they are sick with a sore throat, extra blood is sent to their throat to help repair the damage done by the cold germs. That's why their throat looks red. What's the best way to prevent the spread of germs? Hand-washing! Encourage students to wash their hands often. In particular, this is an effective way to prevent the spread of germs that cause colds. For added incentive, share this fact: Virus germs are so small that millions of them could fit on the period at the end of this sentence.

Learning Center Link

Post a "Feelings" chart at the center. Divide the chart into three parts. On the left, write I Feel Yucky. In the middle, write I Feel So-So. On the right, write I Feel Wonderful. Divide the chart horizontally into five sections, one for each day of the week. Label the days. Invite children to sign in each day according to how they feel. Encourage them to explain their feelings with pictures or words. Use the chart as a guide to understanding your students each day. The information students provide may give you clues to their behavior.

Germ Alert

This lively outdoor game challenges students to avoid germs.

Materials

- ◎ *Germs Make Me Sick* (book or video version)
- ◎ sidewalk chalk
- ◎ game tags (see page 36)

Teaching the Lesson

1 Gather children in a group. Read the book *Germs Make Me Sick* by Melvin Berger (Crowell, 1985), or watch the *Reading Rainbow* video.

2 Brainstorm ways that children can prevent germs from making them sick—for example, by washing their hands before they eat.

3 Make a class set of the game tags. (See page 36.) Write a prevention tip on each of four Prevention tags. Cut apart the tags.

4 Bring the class outside to play a game of Germ Alert. Give each child a tag. (Tape the tags to shirts or punch holes and

string with yarn to make necklaces.) To play, have "Germs" stand in the middle of a large rectangular boundary. Have "Prevention" players scatter around the game area. Have "I'm Healthy" players stand together at one end of the boundary.

5 Explain that when you yell "Germ Alert," the I'm Healthy players must try to get to the other side without being tagged by a Germ. If a child is tagged by a Germ, he or she must sit down until the next round. An I'm Healthy player can tag a Prevention player to be escorted safely to the other side without the risk of being caught by a Germ. Only one person can be escorted at a time by a Prevention player.

6 After playing one round, you may reassign roles and play again.

ACTIVITY Extension Have students trace both their hands on construction paper and cut them out. Have students write their names on their hands, then hang them up on the wall near the bathroom or sink. Encourage children to use the display as a reminder to wash their hands before meals and after using the bathroom.

SCIENCE NOTES

Germs can lie dormant in such places as soil, air, water, food, and on animals, people, and objects until they have a chance to multiply. Germs generally enter the human body through the nose, the mouth, or a break in the skin, such as a cut.

Germ Busters!

You'll have a class of Germ Busters after conducting an experiment that involves seeing how far germs spread when you sneeze or cough, and what happens when you cover your mouth.

Materials

◎ colored construction paper (one sheet for every child)

◎ spray bottles (one for each pair of children: ask children to bring them from home, seek help from fellow teachers, ask for a donation from a local plant store)

◎ tissues

◎ Germ Buster badges (see page 37)

Teaching the Lesson

1. Gather children in a circle. Ask them if they remember what germs do. (*Germs can make you sick.*) Tell students that today they will see just how far germs can spread in the air when people sneeze or cough. They will also discover how to become Germ Busters.

2. Have each child draw a bull's-eye with three concentric circles on his or her paper. (You may wish to provide templates for this.) Ask children to label the circles A, B, and C, with C being the outermost ring.

3. Give each pair a spray bottle filled with water. Explain that the water stands for the germs that come out of people's mouths when they sneeze or cough.

4. Have children stand about three feet away from their partners. One should hold the spray bottle near his or her mouth (with the spray end facing away) and the other should hold the paper in the air with the target facing the sprayer. Make sure the spray bottle nozzles are set to spray a mist. Give the signal to have children squirt water at the target.

5. Ask children to inspect their targets. Then ask them to switch jobs and hold up a clean target (fresh sheet of paper). This time the sprayer holds a tissue over the nozzle of the spray bottle. Give the signal to have them squirt again.

6. Guide children in making connections between spraying the water bottle and sneezing. Ask: *What do you think happens when you sneeze without covering your mouth? What do you think happens when you cover your mouth?* Point out that when they cover their mouths as they sneeze or cough, they're preventing the spread of germs. Make copies of the Germ Buster badges and give one to each child to complete. Children can punch holes at the top and string with yarn to wear.

Literature Connection When you're not feeling well, it's nice to know that you have someone to take care of you. That's the case in *Henry and Mudge Get the Cold Shivers* by Cynthia Rylant (Bradbury Press, 1989). Mudge catches a cold, and Henry showers him with love and attention to help him feel better. Revisit the "I Feel Yucky" poems (see page 33) to make a connection. What makes students feel better when they're sick?

Learning Center Link

Stock a table with paper and art supplies so your students can make Germ Busters signs, such as a picture of a person washing his or her hands. Ask them to come up with slogans, too. Display posters throughout the classroom, and even around the school!

Germ Alert Tags

Prevention Tip _____ _____ _____	**Prevention Tip** _____ _____ _____	**Prevention Tip** _____ _____ _____	**Prevention Tip** _____ _____ _____
Germs	**Germs**	**Germs**	**Germs**
I'm Healthy!	**I'm Healthy!**	**I'm Healthy!**	**I'm Healthy!**
I'm Healthy!	**I'm Healthy!**	**I'm Healthy!**	**I'm Healthy!**
I'm Healthy!	**I'm Healthy!**	**I'm Healthy!**	**I'm Healthy!**

Early Themes: All About Me Scholastic Professional Books

Germk Buster Badges

Name

I'm a Germ Buster!
My germ-busting tip is

Name

I'm a Germ Buster!
My germ-busting tip is

What Makes Me Special?

I n this section your students will learn to appreciate their own unique qualities as well as those of their classmates. They'll discover similarities as well as differences, and they'll find ways to use that knowledge to create a stronger sense of themselves and a stronger sense of classroom community.

SCIENCE NOTES

Hair color, eye color, likes, dislikes…these are just a few of the things that combine to make each of us unique. As children learn more about the ways their bodies work, they can also learn about the less tangible parts of who they are—their personalities, their feelings, their beliefs, and so on.

Who Am I?

Each child is unique. In that sense, the children in your class are all different. Yet they also share many characteristics— for example, they all go to the same school, they all live in the same town or city, and so on. In this activity your students will play guessing games to discover more about the ways they are alike and different.

Materials

- ◎ chart paper
- ◎ Who Am I? activity sheet (see page 43)
- ◎ pencils

Teaching the Lesson

1. Copy the reproducible on chart paper. (See page 43.)

2. Tell students they will be making up riddles about themselves. Explain that a riddle is like a guessing game. Give an example of a riddle—for example, *What has two hands but can't feel anything? A clock!*

3. Fill in the categories on the chart paper using yourself as a model.

4. Give each child a copy of the activity sheet. Ask children to fill in their own papers secretly. (For younger students, you may have to take dictation.)

5. When everyone is finished, collect the papers. Gather children in a group and explain that you'll be reading each riddle aloud without telling whose it is. One person can make one guess after you read each answer. By number five, the identity will be obvious.

6. When you've shared each child's paper, ask: *What are some ways that you are like other students in the class? What are some ways you are not like any other student in the class?*

Literature Connection In *Freckle Juice* by Judy Blume (Bradbury Press, 1971), Andrew will do anything to have freckles on what he believes is a too ordinary face—including trying Sharon's dubious recipe for freckles. When you finish this compelling and humorous look at uniqueness, invite students to concoct their own recipes for Freckle Juice.

Learning Center Link

Set up materials for students to make a collaborative All About Me *class banner. Copy a class set of the template on page 44. When children visit the center, have them complete the poem, then cut out and decorate the picture. Tape children's finished poems together side by side so that the hands are touching. Display the banner to show how special each child is.*

Adapted from 30 Instant Collaborative Classroom Banners *by Deborah Schecter (Scholastic Professional Books, 1999).*

ACTIVITY Extension
Use the information from children's completed "Who Am I?" riddles as the basis of a graph. For example, you might graph hair (color or style), eye color, favorite foods, and letters in initials.

WRITING

Mirror, Mirror

Children look at themselves in a mirror to learn more about who they are on the inside.

Materials

- hand mirrors
- Mirror, Mirror record sheet (see page 45)
- metallic paper or foil

Teaching the Lesson

1. Let children take turns looking at themselves in a hand mirror. Invite them to share things they can tell about themselves by looking in the mirror. Have them record their observations on the mirror-shaped record sheet.

2. Bring children together to discuss their findings. Guide them to recognize that the characteristics they can identify about themselves in the mirror are *physical*—things they can see on the *outside*.

3. Ask: *How can you learn more about who you are on the inside?* Guide children to understand that who they are on the inside includes their personalities, their feelings, their likes and dislikes, and so on. Invite children to share ideas, then complete the right side of the record sheet.

4. Display children's record sheets on a bulletin board backed with metallic paper (or foil).

Literature Connection
What happens when a hippopotamus gets all the features she thinks are important? Find out in *"You Look Ridiculous," Said the Rhinoceros to the Hippopotamus* by Bernard Waber (Houghton Mifflin, 1973). Make a flannel board version of the story to let children use on their own. They can use the pieces to retell the story in their own words, or use them to create new stories.

Learning Center Link

Place hand mirrors, drawing paper, and pencils, markers, and crayons at a learning center. Let children look in the mirrors to create self-portraits. Frame on construction paper and display.

ART/WRITING

Good Days, Bad Days

Sometimes we can be in bad moods, when nothing can make us happy, and sometimes we can be in good moods, where everything is just right with the world. You and your students will make two class Big Books that look at life from both sides of that fence.

Materials

- *Alexander and the Terrible, Horrible, No Good, Very Bad Day*
- chart paper
- large sheets of drawing paper (18 by 24 inches)
- drawing materials (such as watercolor or poster paints, markers, colored pencils)
- Good Days, Bad Days chart (see page 46)

Teaching the Lesson

1. Read the book *Alexander and the Terrible, Horrible, No Good, Very Bad Day* by Judith Viorst (Macmillan, 1972). Ask students if they've ever had days as bad as Alexander's.

2. Make a T chart. On one side write "Bad Days," on the other write "Good Days." Have students discuss things that happened on bad days and good days. Add their comments to the chart paper.

3. Explain that it's okay to be upset, just as it's okay to be happy—they are both feelings, and all people have feelings. Sometimes it's good to express those feelings like Alexander did.

4. Have students choose a good moment and a bad moment in their lives. Invite them to draw pictures of those two moments using a separate sheet of paper for each. Have students write or dictate sentences about each event and add them to their pictures.

5. Bind students' pictures to make two books. Give each book a title, such as *Our Class and the Terrible, Horrible, No Good, Very Bad Day* and *Our Class and the Wonderful, Beautiful, Fantastic, Very Good Day*. (To extend the life of the books, laminate pages before binding.)

6. Go further by giving each child a copy of page 46. Have children complete the chart over a period of a week to learn more about the way they feel.

ACTIVITY Extension Use card stock to make bookmarks with positive messages. Students can write messages on one side of the bookmark and draw pictures on the other side. Have them share their bookmarks with family members or the school library.

Literature Connection Read the poem "If I Were In Charge of the World" from the book of poems by the same name, also by Judith Viorst (Macmillan Publishing Co., 1981). In it a child talks about the things she doesn't like and would get rid of if she could. Compare the poem with *Alexander and the Terrible, Horrible, No Good, Very Bad Day*.

Learning Center Link

Set out paper plates, drawing materials, and a stack of index cards labeled with different emotions or feelings. On one side of a plate, have students write the word for a feeling they've had. On the other side, have them draw a picture to go with the feeling. (Before beginning the activity, you might gather students in a circle and role-play facial expressions related to various emotions.) Hang the plates from the ceiling, or suspend them from a clothesline across the room, so that people can see both sides of the plate.

Put-Up Parade

Encourage children to appreciate one another and give each other "put-ups" instead of put-downs.

Materials

- ◉ chart paper
- ◉ markers
- ◉ tape
- ◉ counters (such as pennies or beans)
- ◉ jar

Teaching the Lesson

1. Ask students if they know what a *put-down* is. (*when someone uses words to make another person feel bad*) Let them share examples. Ask them what they think a *put-up* might be. (*when someone uses words to make another person feel good*)

2. Ask children if they've ever experienced a put-down. Encourage them to talk about how that made them feel. Then ask children if they've ever experienced a put-up. Discuss how that made them feel.

3. Brainstorm different put-ups that students can give one another. Explain that a put-up should mention something specific that a person has done, rather than be a general comment such as "She's nice." Some examples might be: *I like Tanya because she shares the blocks with me. I appreciate Tomas because he helped me stack chairs today.*

4. Show students how to make speech bubbles. (See sample, above right.) Explain that each time a student wants to give a classmate a put-up, he or she can write in a speech bubble, sign his or her name, and tape it up. Have students tape up the put-up notes side by side, across one wall and around the room.

5. At the end of the day, talk about the various put-ups, then count them. For each put-up, place a penny, a bean, or some other counter into the jar. As a class, decide on a special treat or activity when the jar is full.

Literature Connection In *A Chair For My Mother* by Vera Williams (Mulberry Books, 1982), a family fills up a jar with pennies as a way to pay for a big, soft armchair after a fire destroys their furniture. This sweet story supports themes of working together and thinking of others. If you use pennies as counters for your class (see step 5, above), you might ask students if there is a way they could use that money, once the jar is full, to help others.

ACTIVITY Extension After the first day, ask students to predict how many put-ups it will take to fill the jar. Record their answers on a large piece of chart paper. Ask them the same question a week later, once the jar is filled even more. Give them an opportunity to revise their guesses based on the new information. Save the predictions. Once the jar is filled, count the objects. Look back at the chart paper to see how close students came.

Who Am I?

I am a _____ boy _____ girl. (check one)

My favorite food is _____.

My hair is _____.

My eyes are _____.

My initials are _____.

Who am I?

Early Themes: All About Me Scholastic Professional Books

Who Am I?

I am a _____ boy _____ girl. (check one)

My favorite food is _____.

My hair is _____.

My eyes are _____.

My initials are _____.

Who am I?

Early Themes: All About Me Scholastic Professional Books

All About Me!

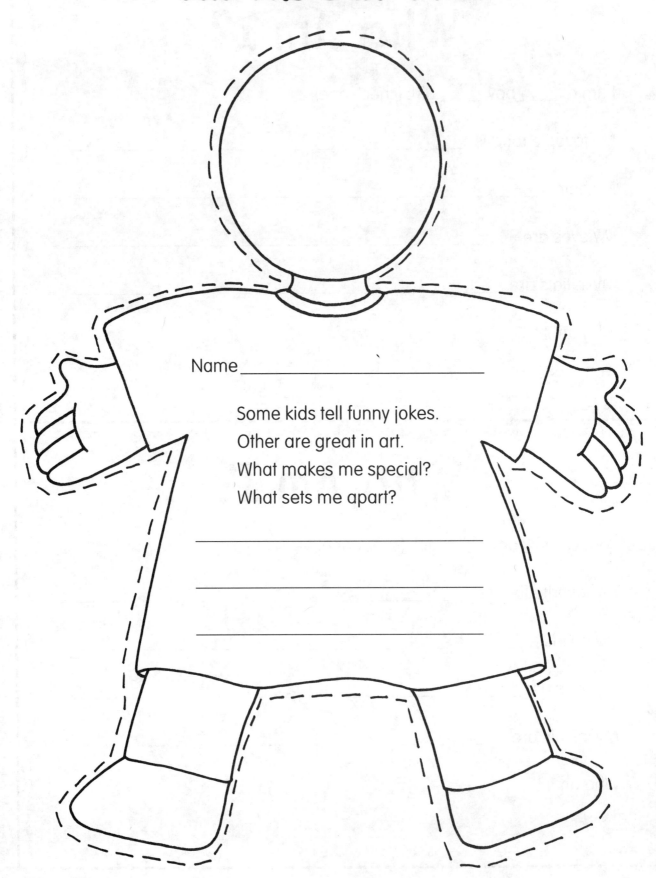

Name_____

Some kids tell funny jokes.
Other are great in art.
What makes me special?
What sets me apart?

_____

_____

_____

Early Themes: All About Me Scholastic Professional Books

Name_____ Date_____

Mirror, Mirror

Things I
know about myself
on the outside

Things I
know about myself
on the inside

Early Themes: All About Me Scholastic Professional Books

Good Days, Bad Days

Tell what happens on good days. Tell what happens on bad days.
Tell how those things make you feel.

Good Days	Bad Days

Early Themes: All About Me Scholastic Professional Books

Health Fair

Let students celebrate and show off what they know about the human body by planning a health fair. As students usher guests around the fair, they can explain what they've learned and point out the different projects they've created. The value of a health fair as an assessment tool is that it allows students to review concepts while also requiring them to synthesize ideas and restate them in their own words.

STEP 1
You're Invited!

Get ready for the celebration by designing invitations that let students revisit what they've learned.

Materials

- ◎ paper
- ◎ template (see page 9)
- ◎ assorted art supplies
- ◎ scissors
- ◎ crayons and markers

Teaching the Lesson

1. Brainstorm information that needs to go on the invitations, such as the name of the event and where and when it's taking place. Write this information on the board or on chart paper.

2. Have children tape sheets of paper together end to end, then fold it accordion-style, as shown. Have children draw a paper-doll shape on the top sheet of paper, making sure the hands and feet meet the sides of the paper. (You may wish to provide a template for this. See sample, page 9.)

3. Guide children in cutting out the pattern, being careful not to cut where the hands and feet meet the sides. (This will keep the accordion fold intact.) Have children complete their fold-out invitations, copying the information from step 1.

TIP: By now, your students have explored the human body inside and outside to learn about the ways their bodies work and what makes each of them special. Let students demonstrate their knowledge by completing the KWL charts. (See page 8.) Display the charts at the health fair.

STEP 2
Planning the Fair

Set up student-led information stations for the fair.

Materials

- ◎ posterboard
- ◎ crayons, markers
- ◎ assorted art supplies

Teaching the Lesson

1. Divide students into five groups of experts. Each group will be responsible for covering one of the questions or topics included in the unit. (If you've covered additional material, adjust the size of the groups to include this.)

2. Have students in each group review the material in their folders and journals. Guide them in deciding what to include at the health fair station. Suggestions include:

- ◎ Display KWL Charts. (See page 8.)
- ◎ Sing "Make New Friends." (See page 22.)
- ◎ Set up "touch boxes." (See page 27.)
- ◎ Play the game Germ Alert. (See page 34.)
- ◎ Display the collaborative banner. (See page 39.)
- ◎ Read aloud poetry. (See page 31.)
- ◎ Share "Who Am I?" riddles. (See page 39.)
- ◎ Display Germ Busters posters. (See page 35.)

3. Have children prepare materials for their stations and make banners identifying their questions or topics.

4. Set up stations in the classroom or another large space and welcome your visitors!